born to cry

laura sermeño

what matters most is how well you walk through the fire.

-Charles Bukowski

Contents

1 Act of Escaping — 4
2 Succulence — 7
3 Miguel — 10
4 Hit Me — 13
5 Missing — 15
6 Mod Womxn — 17
7 Not My Friend — 19
8 Before I Could Say It To Your Face — 21
9 You Were Mine — 22
10 Xican@ For Short — 23
11 Awake At Night — 25
12 Mi desgracia académica — 27
13 bi-polar-ness — 29
14 Lupita — 33
15 So that she is not forgotten — 35
16 Orchid — 38
17 cuerpo — 40
18 I am not — 43
19 here again — 45

20 Don't Vote	47
21 Love itself	51
22 Strawberry Moon	52
23 Angel	54
24 Going	57
25 Soul	59
26 To Los Angeles	61
27 Alex	64
28 Want	66
29 Against Me	68
30 the bastard who cheats	70
31 The Truth	72
32 Protect Women	75
33 ode to teotihuacan	77
34 Stars who shine bright explode	79
35 for she taught me love was abuse	81
36 Interstitial in your life	83
37 menstruación	84
38 i miss you, grandma	85

39 I see because you gave me vision — 86
40 adivinando divinidad — 88
41 awake at the sight of you — 89
42 antonio — 92
43 delicate — 94
44 On loving myself— — 96
45 Waste — 97
46 Mamá — 98
47 We made life — 99
48 question — 100
49 mutual manipulation — 101
50 Nothingness — 103
acknowledgements

Act of Escaping

My pulsing temple screams out anger
and my beating heart wants to make
stardust of the tears that stain my
cheeks from thoughts of you.
my swelling oculi — tired of sad —
question my very motivation to get better because
why quit the fight when I jab so good?
I thrive in confrontation and maneuver away
from inward speculation. introspection.
Questioning, questioning my participation
in what happens to me because
thrown into the universe, I've been receiving
injustice since conception.
because if you hurt too, you'd be in that
waiting room with me. your silence bequeaths
my wanting. Who wants passive? I want action.
I want alive and in-your-face coming 'atcha in 3D
live from my grandmother's living room with
rawness to prove — I SCREAM YOUR NAME.
Stop evading my echoing truth.
I SCREAMED, "NO!" in that living room my

grandparents bought with their
immigrant money. The same exact place
I bit your cheeks and
that's how I've come to believe
that no one respects that I am mine.
Even my enchantment belongs to me. Even
my destructive darkness. And it's hard.
But because my journey is so damn
inconceivable to others, it makes me want me
more than I want anything else.
This nagging in my noggin is louder —
and growing because I feed it concern;
I let it speak to me because I've manufactured the words.
I give my tragic side a voice because I am unafraid
of what I am revealing; that is so much more than
my cold skin illuminated by the moon through slits in my
curtains.
My inner self; much more vulnerable than what
resides in my inner thighs. I can spread before I really
open
cus it is easier; I am easier to love physically
and I know this — and I play this — and I take advantage.
And I come out on top.

Oh, how I always lose.

I've got this act down to an art.

Succulence

Crisp and chilled, out in the world.
Not quite like the Westside
because the stares and the neck-breaking
behavior occurs incessantly.
I liked the walk to your house
and felt the pace of my heart increase as I broke in
my Mexican sandals. These huaraches brought me to your
mother's greenhouse and I hid from your sister behind
a hedge because she would think I was overdressed.
I *was* overdressed because I'm not effortless.
I don't feel naturally compelling.
So I snuck inside and played with
Sadie, every now and then knocking for you, while
entertaining myself with a toy I found resting on
your mother's patio table. Nice house.
Beautiful plants adorning the front yard — inspired by
your
sister's passions. Turns out you were lunching with your
Abuelita in her backhouse. Her couches were lined with
White doily-like cloth and her cooking paralleled my
nana's.

No other Abuelita has compared in the past. She stayed beside us,
filling our bowls with fideo and frijoles paired with icy glasses
coated with frost, filled with jamaica. Y los limones.
Me ofrecieron aguacate pero a mí no me gustan. I
preferred a pomegranate. And you looked good. You grew up.
No longer silly six-year-olds, we
mused about our devastating writing experiences. Sentence structure?
What's that? Your big sister opened up to me and I,
bent on making the night fun, got her to buy us alcohol by first fattening her
up with a cool, frozen yogurt. She chose strawberry flavor with jelly,
coconut flakes, almond slices, kiwi, mochi balls and lechera.
I demanded plain yogurt when the machine quit working and loaded
my serving with mango, strawberry, mochi, rainbow sprinkles and that
oddly reminiscent, and disturbingly addictive, lechera.

We sat around in a circle
and I licked my lipstick and the tastiness off my candy-
coated ice cream. Then we smoked. Blunted. I was
down for your bong and much
more, but not yet. I know you're a boy cus your
buddies are over all day
and I gotta keep busy with your sister. Making salad.
We collaborated on dinner, and gained buzz from our
ale - infused with orange zest and slices.
Spinach, gorgonzola cheese, pomegranate, pear, sugar
and bee-pollen encrusted walnuts comprised our salad
and mixed and melded with a
pomegranate balsamic vinaigrette that consorted
together to make my insides somersault and rejoice.
Food! Conviviality! We ate so much and that's
how I know I can be happy again. You're bringing
back my appetite — but
I should warn you about my vicious thirst.

Miguel

Clenched face, cracking spine —
Undo my wariness of you.
My nerves guard me from my
fluttering agony revisiting me
ever-so-often to remind me that I am
not mine. I gave myself away much
too soon and now a hollow abyss
remains. I long to see your face
and brush a kiss onto your cheek
the way I used to miss waiting for
my mother to get home from work.
I owe it to her to be strong now
to let go and be unmoved by your
existence. Angel, my precious love,
I will never forget the fluorescent,
jubilant light you brought to
my life. I just miss your heart
so much and depending on what
music I listen to, I can feel our
souls intertwining out of a common
yearning. I'm sad for me, I'm

sad for you and that we both
hurt because what we wanted the most
is no good for us now. You know,
Things would have been different
and we might've made it. I still
cling onto that idea and hopelessly
remember all of our times together.
Like spending our last night in
your old apartment — with one
cover between the both of us on
that wooden floor. Or our time at
Santa Monica beach and how
you held onto me tightly and
became my rock. I feel lost. I
feel fooled. I lost my love. I
fooled you. I remember your
mouth locking onto mine and
devouring that freshness and love
I put out. You consumed it all.
You consumed my entire will power
and ate all my charm. I accept
it, I still remain alive and
stubbornly so. I desire to get

over you any way that I
can. Can you stop? Can you
forget me? I know I made your
day better most days. I know I
made love to you with all of my
heart and passion. With desire
and beauty, I held you right.
You were close to me and forever
imprinted on my soul. Our problem
being that neither of us backs
down and we were devoted to winning at
any cost. I must say I am defeated;
though, I'm not sure I'm the only loser.

Hit Me

Like holding onto something that would prefer to
Remain untouched. I promise, I promise not to get close.
Oh, I've made that mistake again, expecting to blurt an
Unapologetic "sorry." That's not lamentable. I'm not
Sorry I couldn't help touching you after I'd sworn not
to.
I'm fine with inviting you over after saying I never wanted
To see you. It's true, I made those promises long ago and
With little and fading intent to follow through. I can't say I
Cared too much that you were ugly since you reflected
My feelings of myself and your insecurity matched my
Insanity. I want these to be the last lines I write to you, but
Like my scars, you remain imprinted all over and around my
Soul — no matter how much I want you to disappear. Hey, now
You know how you make my stomach jolt and my heart crash

And my pen fly. How I react in such a timely manner. I'm not
Embarrassed - I don't feel bad about this, I mean I cry incessantly
But I still, still, still cannot regret performing oh so long for you
And putting on a grand show, in which I star as the central fool.
Miguel, you put it on me — you give it to me — and you take it away.
And it feels, and it felt, like love and every consequent action
Arose from a repudiation, an obsession and an exclamation
Of me projected onto you. I sort of wish I knew what kind of
Investigations you launched for me because I'm sure you're
Spying somehow; as much as my curiosity fuels my innermost
Thoughts and desires in respect to you, you're worse.
Where do you stalk? Are you watching me? For everyday you
Perturb my thoughts, I shall haunt your life times two.

Missing

It is happening again.
I can feel it in my face, on my neck,
And my ears are burning once more.
Is he thinking of me? Does he speak of
Me tonight? In this instance are we both
Sharing liquid telepathy streaming down
Our faces? Oh, and the happening is
Everlasting and imprinted on the lines in
My face, on the lines of my fingers and
Figure and especially in my deep and hollow
Sighing. In the shivering of my chin, you can
Tell the holding back is happening and throbbing
At my raw neck. Raw because during sleep
I utter things like "it's your fault, it's your fault -
You ruined everything." Or so says my brother.
I think he relates — especially when immediately
After these utterances, my subconscious
Forces laughter from my throat. I have to feel
Better somehow and my body knows it.
So, my dreams are splendid and soaked with
Everything about you, just like the paper I

Write on. Sopped and breakable as can be,
The paper I write upon has nothing on me.
I am the wet and shattered one, no one wishes
To speak of, even I want to sweep up I'm done
With the keep-up and my tormented mind.

Mod Womxn

Dastardly you grip onto me
and my infatuations with
men incomplete. Men so fragile,
they hook onto my smiles
and fluttering flirtations.
I dare to reject you
and all of your manifestations.
But me in this silky sheer
shirt leaves you breathless.
Panting and trembling, let your
daze consume you. Or me?
Your gaze eats my face! My
face, in public, is on display.
As feminine bodies navigate
through worldly spaces: hair,
jewelry, maquillaje,
clothing drips off, strips
off, slips off. We're
naked. Bare bodies burgeoned
by boyish biases. Sexy.
Sex, see? Sex, me?

Me. Me! My sex is mine and
You are not invited. Your
optical undressing of my sexiness
revolts me and I am holding
in my disgust. Respect that this excess of
sex suppresses, represses,
oppresses, the visual mystery
and beauty of the human body.
If you take, I cannot give.
When you rake, green cannot
Live! Stay true to the
Femme experience cus I live
this. Pride aside, where is
the love?

Not My Friend

So much I let go unsaid.
It's in the sweet and fleeting
pauses that I can see your chilled
heart in — and it torments me to
know it's not me for you.
Because we rip into each
other with each unspoken feeling,
it separates us and agonizes me.
Though I didn't come here for
this — I meant for you to fill me
and add pure notes of bliss
into my sappy nightmare life.
Go ahead and push me. It's
dizzying; this stinking, sinking catastrophe.
This ink to paper makes thoughts
concrete but won't urge me to speak
to you. We don't belong together.
It's too fucking difficult and right
from the start, you wanted to freeze.
Against my will, I'll stay because I can't
breathe the ending I foresee.

I can't take apocalypse to surface;
I can but only take the ride and
feel our distracting magic.

Before I Could Say It To Your Face

Begin at the break of dawn.
I'd like to pause, prolong
a gentle look, a sweet caress.
How to capture this in couplets?
I want to scream it off a balcony,
but I wouldn't say it to your face; oh! the agony.
I don't know what we are, but somehow that's better
than knowing we are nothing.
Better than falling, longing, beckoning for something.
You say it - but do you mean it?
You do it - but do you feel it?
If you're going to fall,
fall hard or not at all.
Let go
— while the stakes are low.
I'm heartbroken, and I can't connect, maybe mad
but mean no disrespect.

You Were Mine

gazing slightly in your direction and
catching your stare; I see that we
both beckon the love that fills us.
I quickly shift my eyes and almost
subconsciously turn my knees towards
your body — and with that I seem to
scream for you to hold me tighter.
with each accidental side-stare
we fall into this lovely game, the
one where I play coy and you
become the quick-wit boy.
there's no telling where it's
going but the repetitive
shiftiness gets the best of
both of us and we just lay there
in a giggle-fit and sigh peacefully
until morning breaks.

Xican@ For Short

Crashes, crashing of culture and language...
Latin, lambda, lengua...
Nahuatls, nalgas, and nacas...
Amnesty, amalgamate...
Histories of conquest and throes of passion
Synthesize and integrate, assimilate, create
a new "human," a "mestizo," or person often described
as "neither here nor there"; neither American nor
Mexican; neither English nor Spanish... so?
I beg, I ask, who are we? Who is she?
A "people" with no fixed racial category on those
government documents...
Folk who either transcend or essentialize race
altogether,
or do neither.
Who's our mother and how can we, the neither
Mexican nor Americans, preserve her identity?
Are we the reincarnation of mexicanas longing
to love one another?! Queers within our own skin?
Internalized as different, marked by deviance...
of the body, of the ACT, of the aggressive lust

embedded in some code.

Conquistadores, communists, catholics.

Ever stratifying and demarcating each other

with each other, through each other, by each other

but rarely for each other...

Confused and masked by religion, social acceptance,

and historical preservation....

WE. ARE. LOST.

Awake At Night

It's ok when I don't know what to do
In the middle of the nights, that sting of self-realization
That was more bitter than you bit through.
The nights catch my normal everything stops and lately
I'd forgotten I was broken.
Lifted highly and revered for getting out and doing the thing
That kept me from being a mother. Being looked at by somebody
Who's something, and my life is a something.
The ins and outs, the quickie, and the sleeping-in with
The covers over my eyes, not my nostrils;
With the sheets that aren't yours or mine.
In control and out of time; quickly onto the next diversion —
I'm pretty sure I didn't say you could see that part.
I'll stay quiet.
Turn away. I'm absolutely in need to say that you can't call me
Human — you hardly have any evidence suggesting.

Come on laughter, you don't get the point, we said
Be serious.
Those nights when I'm crying a lot and I'm
Scared of myself because I know I'm quiet a lot. Back then I
Saved all the cool words and had thought-banks filled
With words like hate.

Mi desgracia académica

La academia es un lugar de falta de respeto.
Es oblivio en el sentido secreto porque a fundar el genio es
Ponerlo en un lugar sin creatividad. Por supuesto las
Ganas de salir adelante es adecuado para cualquier persona
Que anda de la búsqueda de novedades como la pinche posteridad.
Encuentros, audiencias, la promoción del único que tiene
Sustancia. Es perfecto embarazarse de esas ideas y hacerse alguien quien
Pone un acto enfrente de la gente. Oooo. Ahhhhhhh.
Gente, gente, gente. Por favor. No se pongan así.
Para qué sirvo yo, sino para ofender a esas mismas audiencias
Captadas por la ruptura fingida. No hay chiste en simplemente
Decirnos, "Mira, esto es diferente de lo de antes, nosotros no
Estamos bebiendo de la teta de la academia, somos

únicos, ¿no ven?

La población entera, ignorante."

bi-polar-ness

When I can't sleep at night, it sends me into a spiral...
I'm thinking: "Is tonight the night I get sick again and forget what chaos I create for myself?"
"Is this the night I set myself back for months, again?"
My anniversary of my hospital stay just passed.
May 30th, 2013.
I can't tell you how triggering this looming demarcation of my mental split has been.
I can't express nicely and succinctly for you how I've methodologically kept striving for my
health every day.
Doing everything for myself and pausing the external.
Hit RECORD.
Bring me my favorite scent of lavender and rub it all around.
Check my heart rate and begin thinking of blank — of white — of black.
Don't focus so much on the color, focus on the blank
-ness of submitting to your primal needs.
Your body is resetting and let's visit your subconscious
-how upsetting.

And I don't know what I'm getting
AT or FROM — this writing is dumb;
this flimsy first attempt at some creativity.
Because the passivity and sterility of the hospital is
barely fading from my short term memory
and harvesting its impact into my cerebral entity.
For a lifetime.
There — forever — so I can recall and redirect
reconstruct what happened and peel the band-aid
slowly.
Slower.
Slower.
Pace your breathing.
Go into fetal.
Maybe start praying the religious literature you've
memorized.
I was socialized to pray before bed and hope to god I'd
just never wake up.
"Ave Maria Purisima!"
I like the way it sounds.
I do enjoy going back to my childhood and self-
soothing to sleep.
Sleep, you escape me and I chase you, but I don't want

you.

"Dios te salve, Maria, llena eres de gracia, El Señor es contigo. Bendita tú eres entre todas las

mujeres, y bendito es el fruto de tu vientre: Jesús. Santa Maria, Madre de Dios, ruega por

nosotros, los pecadores, ahora y en la hora de nuestra muerte. Amén."

I don't mean to preach, but I want to profess that for me in times of duress,

I pray to false figures who momentarily treasure my burdens and hold them for certain.

Hold them when my strength's not workin' and when life is jerkin' me.

Here's a snippet from an email I sent to a sympathetic TA during my first manic episode, just one

year ago:

"It's quite the ordeal to exist within a system imposed to challenge your intelligence and box you

in on a timeline... I am just being squished... by the system that glorifies the matter between my

ears that don't matter to them... My main point is... This is out of our control and I'm under control and out of control in my mind."

Pause.

And if there's ever a time when I'm bordering the line of a stable or manic mind, it's when I'm sending stupid emails

about how I can't do anything academic on time.

Because my time is mine, and it's all spread out and around.

It's all groovy for me up until you try to teach in a top-down manner because I don't have the

etiquette necessary.

I'm not a passive educational mercenary.

I'm not sorry I don't fit in.

I'm not surprised I'm yet another "crazed female" and a brown one at that.

I'm this, that, and the other, and just another example of how institutional and academic

timelines cramped MY style SO much I lost IT.

It didn't lose me and look, see, I'm here, it's clear and apropos to say

I've come back after a delay

to retrieve a paper that exclaims

U-C-L-A.

Lupita

Giving into the beauty of death
and your eyeliner catastrophe resembles a mess.
You're letting go of the grip
of life, and I do not blame it.
If you gave up on something else instead, you'd be here with me
and not buried in Guadalajara.
Over there, you're happily returning to the earth
and I'm writing my feelings out on dirt.
I think you're going to get it, or I might send
you messages through sand when I'm buried in my mother tierra.
Like consumption of self and the ego,
I cannot swallow the definitive power of grandma death;
she's old, I wish you could've beaten her down.
Laughter, laughter, laughter
Because of the joy you were
and always will be.
What a grace
What a person, and really no one can forget you.

I was a beautiful child in your eyes.
I had innocence retained and reflected
off your crystal Tapatio eyes/we
Both glistened.

So that she is not forgotten

You can retrace the places she's
shared her victories/
Of memories long-lasting,
Happiness finally held well.
With empty streets holding space for
Dreams passed, lands with other
meanings now.
Remember that she jumped up and
down when excited.
The staggering, skinny pine tree she
brought home in the third grade
grows by her grave.
Her name debated —she accepts what
familia tells her to be.
A plant, a friend, a breath of
Fresh, that's what she loves.
I forget her rarely, but these
things will always mean her.
In all things —kindness, in all
actions —a spark.
An echoing, billowing laughter, the

roar above mountains, it leads

Coyotes to the truth.

Largeness throughout in meandering

desert paths, the ways to your

heart were always tucked away/

behind cactus plants flowering blue dreams.

Children met you and always loved you —

Such a fun aura how

young you once were.

Retrace her steps back to

great grimy streets — wherever there's art,

there she will be.

So you can make sure in your growing

and years passing, that you can put

down someone worth remembering, worth the

pen, paper and strife/ with furrowed-brow confusion,

sometimes you'll

look like her.

A sudden reenactment that gives you

heart floatin', my dear child who questions/ now you

can know…

She loved poems, stickers, good shoes

and pillows.

On days that it rained, it could be
so stormy inside yet sometimes
she'd face it with no sweater with to
hide. full smiles on and face up,
the girl ready to soak.
That's who she was, all that she showed
but with secrets tenfold.
She loved more and more daily
Not scared to explode.

Orchid

The long vastness of the night and the anticipation
Of high school prom/ as the best fucking night to come.
However, feelings of dismemberment or/ of out-of-body existence travel
Tainted the night.
The night tainted by afternoon, after rude,
After obtuse behavior — teenagers, emotions so big, nothing will let them dissipate.
I'm in full promzilla mode, snapping left and right, left and right
I snap my retorts, complaints, and anxiety-hate.
Right here with this fuck up, it's all me doing all bad.
I'm the fucking jackass/ until I'm browsing the web on my
high school sweetheart's phone — an unknown number texts/
I'm flipping my shit internally.
I'm all — who's this? I text her: 'who are you looking to speak to?'
She spells your name all the way right, the way

someone would only if they/

Knew you.

I'm like, 'oh, where do I know you from?'

And she all

'we met at the farmer's market, and went out twice.'

Commence full-blown, cheated-on meltdown, fully

fully fully multiplied by

Motherfucking promzilla mode, already in full swing.

And let it swing I did, I had never hit someone,

But I did, I punched him so hard in his big arm.

He was 6' 4" and nearing 300 pounds — he could take it.

After all, he begun my real challenge for me

unwittingly — after

My corsage orchid tattered, after right arm battered,

After no prom dancing, and after new life waiting/

After four years passed, I write this down.

cuerpo

hand small, fingers skinny and straight, hairy knuckles
my own hand, thin, long thumb
only the pinky like you abuelito
y no se endereza — it's a crooked pinky.
your other fingers, though. they're ravaged by time
more so than other elderly.
your whole hand disfigured mine
just at the end
just at the pinkies.
your coraje shows, you carry it.
tu nunca fuiste nada para mi 'belito.
tu nunca me hablabas.
y no comparto nada más con nadie más.
I don't even have similarities to anyone on my mom's
side —
I don't know father's side
those identical strangers, unknowns
With my features.
I only have something in common with you,
on mom's side.
tenemos un parecido yo y mi mamá, pero nada más.

present father, absent mind you were

never there for her.

you answered serious questions with redundant jokes

you laughed when no one

knew why

you added confusion, hurt and all the hidden stories

through your diversions.

i don't know you at all

not never will i

this summer

through your brother

i learned some more

that winding jaliciense mountain paths

you memorized jaggedness

half conscious in your trailer

i'll hold onto that as some sort of connection

as i've memorized my jagged finger,

wrought with lines

old lady hands

without knowing, unconscious of our connection

but winding with the haphazardness

of your empty words

rotting laughter

mighty eyes

mighty roar
fading man in his head winding all the things
flustered by memories
of living life without a path
going this way and that and dragging
the whole family with you.
not provider, not lover
not supporter, not friendly
not a memory with you
worth mentioning
nothing I can remember but re-routed stories.
never been to where you want to
lead the conversation
never wanting to know
why
just
so
confused.
how am i like you?

I am not

What I'm not perhaps won't reinforce what I am.
That's someone who gives a fuck about
The world.
I am not the grim reaper disguised as a güera.
I am not the friend you confide in
Who will reveal you.
I am not occult and tricking.
I am so not a white girl appropriating gang typeface
and calling themselves 'Sad Girl' with it.
I am not a piece of meat or someone who eats pieces of meat.
I am not a conundrum.
I'm here in one digestible piece.
I make sense.
I am not ruffled feathers, yet I'm not to be bothered
with bullshit.
I am not stagnant and festering with all that I'm not.

With what I claim and what I own, I'll let you know —
I feel good.
As a child of dichotomous, colonial human

contradictions, I'll still assert that I am not one.

I am many in one; there's greatness within my historical bones. I am not my opposite. I am not all put together.

I am not a mistake, and I'm not my parents' mistakes. I am their successes.

I am not confusing, a puzzle, hard to get

— I am known.

here again

The elevator music and the impersonal "care."
Coffee elevates my heart rate
which fucks with my blood pressure
— is that right?
I'm here for my head, my mind and
not for my health, though.
Are they inextricable?
Mental health — that's a trend.
My mind wandered to no man's land
and I was dumped into some sterile place
stripped of life.
Compassion so far gone but I see
it off in the distance if I squint.
These nurses are not your friends;
They're nosy babysitters.
Oh, you're sad today?
Oh, you'd like to floss?
We better monitor that before you make a mistake
to try to take your own life.
But I'm not even here because of that.
I do want to live

but your constant fear and impositions about
suicide are making things worse for me.
I'll stay extra days/
extra weeks
in this hole of hell
Because I won't admit I lost anything at all.
Not to you.
Not to doctors.
Not to anyone/
my mind is mine to do with as necessary.
I don't freak at the parts that squeak from overuse.
And all of you who whisper I'm crazy,
fuck yous.
You obviously do not understand genius in overload mode.
You do not get *Alice in Wonderland*.
You were never ready for the artist life.
Back off from this episode/
it gives me a hell of a lot more to write.

Don't Vote

With or without our politics
This history repeats
There are no more Civil Rights
Rights only secured by movement
The struggle to agree to struggle
Together.
And the dirty downside to believing
we're not family fighting oppression.
Because it's easier to attack mother
Rather than the hand that writes
The paycheck.

Our money

savings accounts

creating further divide

If thousands separate us, then we
dine in different restaurants
Ignorant to the billionaires

who break bread with one another
Over contemplations of furthering their
World
Domination.

The brutality of picking a puppet to
distract us from the occult truth!
Let us be horrified by American
Oligarchy….

Will you believe it even if the
strings of our presidential puppets are
Exposed in plain sight?
Will you believe it if the puppet
masters string the puppets to mouth
The words?

"There is no democracy here — you are all
mind-controlled monkey machines."
And I'm not a puppet, so I'll tell
You the truth.
Right in your mouth-open face.
It's time to get angry but don't

Displace it towards me —
Follow the money, count the
Receipts because they all trace back.

What will it take to wake up,
America?
Will it be when there's hunger in our streets?
When our systems fall apart as the world swallows us
entirely
— making us succumb to her
for our negligence?
Maybe when it's too late, when
we're suffering in the conditions we've
pushed our global family to live
through — we might want to try.
Maybe when

complacency dries up with the last
drop
of drinkable water.

All the seeds of sorrow this country
blindly plants

Will grow as a cancer.
It's reached Cambodia,
Palestine, Bangladesh, India, Mexico
and more…
It's going to get you, too.

The cancer will totally consume
Me as well.

There must be something to do.

Love itself

Swooping winds that stir up and tempt me.
An ensuing flame, a welcome fire that
Doesn't burn because we crave it. Those
Gentle breaths like a sweet caress that
I cannot give up. A smile growing, a
Calm knowing, that you are my life's
Peace to cherish. And in the chaos that
emerges in your radical pursuits, you
Will be met. From elements distilled
by nature, like us, I plead that
You compliment me. A rushing force
from earthly heavens has found
Ceaseless energy from the heat. Our
Faces glowing, warm palms now
Touch… in my heart you give me
Life.

Strawberry Moon

In warm times and birthdays looming
with the eager shift of salvation
And a craving, most likely
Dipped in chocolate.

I love you for both of your sides,
Ripe and blushing red
With dark, moldy bits to echo
Your darkness.

You can fold your sides like origami,
And often I can only view
The good.

You can lie a thousand times,
and in earnest I'm blinded
By the radiance of fresh fruit to behold.

My insatiable curiousness picks at your seeds
As you leave treasures behind
through mazes made

By weaseling.

Children bond with you and give you
their troubles because the smiles
You give each one creates
Big love bubbles.

Angel

And in the moment I feel the haggard pain —
Exactly where my body was chipped away.
I can't explain this ghost pain
Other than with something once
Grew there.
And was ripped away from me.
And that started with my
Planning and imagining of a family
With you and me.
I tried to give us new life
and bring one up for us.
I tried so hard, my inside burst.
I tried to give myself a love brand
new — both a love outside of me and you,
and a love combined.
I wanted to give myself a new
Challenge of how to manage a small child.
How to make them in all the ways we were made. And
I still want them.

I gave a whole part of myself — yes, I

neared the realm of death for wanting
a new life; it gave me scars and
torments for forcing it through.

You gave me worries and earthly requests
but I reminded you that women's
work could not be bothered by reality's stresses.

I am a whole divinity searching for
you — to mother. I am my angel's
efforts to keep me alive and prosper
and multiply. I am the giver and
all I've had to offer was love and
life. I am here still patient and
breathing with the blessings of life. I
am a mother, a real one, despite all my
losses. My children, the spirits, will
find their right time. Their echoes, my
laughter, have fun through the
night. My love, his love, we give you
by right.

You will inherit this ache, our smiles

and our fears

But you, you are all the love that

I am. And we, we wait to meet you

again.

Going

You are blazing a path ahead
as the sun kisses your shoulders
as it shocks dead brush into fire
that, "storm brewing behind you…"

You, as the fire too hot to carry
Too hot for cowards.

Blazing forward — the storm fails
to dampen your trails.
Onward, you trust what you do not know
more than what you do.
In a full spectacle of change,
you blame the storm for catalyzing
This movement.

Your way needs no bendiciones,
and your mother may never say goodbye.
It may be just as likely you'll
Meet at your graves.
The road you are choosing needs

No good intentions.
The road needs you to move.

Your seasons are long
and this is your second bloom
— remontant, defiant
Growing and true…

Soul

If, when delving into my soul, I get lost, don't come and find me.
If I'm scared to take the deep plunge into myself — push me, and I'll say I dove alone.

Though I may be terrible at understanding the human mechanics that compose me... I am finished.
Though I am unaware of all that binds me in my mind... It makes sense.

And on days like these — when I spend every waking second running around, avoiding my thoughts yet accomplishing everything I set out to do

— let me know

That I am a do-er.
That I am completely self-sufficient.
That I am a genius with charms who can stretch a buck.
That I am building myself while teaching myself.

the lessons that were missed.

On days like these — playing hookie from "responsibilities" — missing "school" or "work" — these days were better savored. These days I lay in a bed of roses.
 These days I tease the hard workers... playing in the street with my bike running circles.

On these days reserved for magical discovery, my soul asks for "more wonder… "

I say: "of course, right away."
I say: "I know just what you like."
I say: "go to the moon."

And the best days are unplanned:

> They're plan-as-you-go
> They're better this way
> They're nutrition for the heart.

To Los Angeles

In the humble rumbling
of my plans
and as they open to change

I still want to confront my/our contradictions
and since "retaliation does not wait..."
I am feeling the heaviness of your hatred.

"In the midst I think of you
and how it used to be."
my body creaks from
Our misfortunes.

Love, my love, given and gained…
The overflowing/outpouring
los ambos amores que he tenido
las mujeres que me han conocido…
In Los Angeles, among the stars I
Am home; among Las Lunas
 my star grows.

I am no longer sad/*how can I be?*
I am destined and plotting
all the dots in my constellation

Mi fuego burns brightly tonight
The rumbo in my mind hums gently
since "we have never been safe,"
but we have been trained.

My body/spirit/mind fight in this
exercise — my soul release into
my path
my unknown
my paving of new home
my forging new life
my destino in the light
my pasado in the dark,
In the chapter I am closing.
In goodbyes turned good morning.

My Los Angeles… mi Aztlán…

pedacito de cambio…

myth turned reality.

In the city heat of fictitious design;

My pueblo, I love you,

we'll meet in due time.

Alex

we're waged and engaged in an emotional war

one of push and pull

And the yo-yo games I'm forced

To accept as part of my life.

Combatting my sadness — finding this way

Finding his body at your doorstep.

greeting me with the love I missed.

For the love I long for cannot be this

What this is…

What this mess morphed into.

I am "fighting sadness" with his kiss

I am finding the girl within

I am hearing my favorite band with my favorite man

I am folding into him and

He reminds me of who I was

He remembers my hips and

He lingers on my soul.

He's my cherished/my special hope

And I know I missed the boat.

I know it just like most how we
shall crumble and
I won't begin again through
the romance of my past…

I was feeling so alone and at home
At your kissing of my spine
I was dancing in my mind
thinking not of consequences, but only of you.
I was passionate at the finish
enveloped in your smell.

I was kissing at the air, believing you were there.
I was loving every moment
suspended by your breath.
Because that truth is waiting.

Want

Thank you for the kisses
I am the butterfly misses
I am living on side cheek kisses
Unwary, and only holding onto
glimmers and rays of breakthroughs.
Give me all the love you were born with
All of it in abundance.
Displace, with me, your romantic
Longings
Our romantic evenings
with just hugs
just talks
just rubs
in just the right places
Be comfortable with this
Fall into my kiss
Fade into my man and hold
me by the small of my back.
If I can smile through a
lie so pure
If I can muster the energy

for you
If I can teach of the
pain in bosoms
If you can withstand
the labor
cum delayed
heart's gratification...
Throbbing in want...
Then I can try
with you.

Against Me

my karma has come to attack me
and it has me weak —
Reaching for any substance or bottle
that can calm my spinning thoughts.

I've been an awful woman to my femme
comrades — I have lied and cheated
With their stupid men with my stupid body.

I have been buried by my own men
The ones I give power to every time
I let something enormous pass by under
My nose.

This is my karma for my stupid, selfish
Behavior. There are valid, disturbing reasons
For the onslaught of lessons I face today.
I looked at their faces — Daisy and
Ashley, and I do not know who else — I
Lied. To protect me. To protect their
Stupid men. To feel some carnal validation.

To know what I already knew. To prove nothing
to nobody but myself. To relish in the
dirty thoughts, the pleasant familiar self-
Satisfaction of my secrets…

the bastard who cheats

he says it's because of me and
My flirting.
He's lousy and does this to every woman —
But this is me. I demand respect.

He says I made him do it
Because I broke his heart. He says
I cheated first. I didn't,
But I wish I had.

I wish I was a bastard just like you:
No conscience, filthy sheets, self-
satisfied in mediocrity. As human
as the best and the worst of us.
As rotten as the worst thoughts, your
Parents had for each other with
Their emotions spilling frothiness from
the sides of their mouths.

I cannot be a bastard like you. I've
got reason, logic, and

Meaninglessness on my side. I have
got a sense of self twice as big
as your dick.
I've the face of an angel: I am
shining in god's glory. I am bad men's
worst nightmare; I am the shadow
and the knife here to end
Bastards like *you*.

The Truth

Well I am searching for
a truth that doesn't
Start with you.
A truth deeper than a
snoop — a privacy given and
not taken on a whim.
I am searching for a life
within, I am looking for a
tear of truth.
A lie cannot be where a tear
has lain.

A tear can only reveal what's
pained within.

A tear as the final stronghold
that anger has — your weeping
after no breathing, holding in
your infant rage.
That anger
enveloping key parts of yourself.

You, unable to give those parts
names and your mother who swears
she's never known these feelings.

Those feelings being scribbled
in your blood centuries ago.

That sweet release of liquid
excreting is more truthful
than mamá — those tears are
paths, reminders of what your
ancestors have known. Your tears
are courage, sweet love, they are
what you are — and the anger, a
gift, and the destruction, merely
masks what's inside.

As shocked and embarrassed as your
emotion sways you — it is a whole
existence of longing
it is a whole book worth memorizing
it is the blueprint to a tunnel
so revealing/so buried within you

the tears, they come as companions/
they come to guide you.

The tears, they are free, unwanting
and abundant.

Follow them, go with them.
They are the truth.

Protect Women

They will ask why women need shields
And if we decide to respond, we'll say:
"Warriors will always come protected."

We must protect each other to protect ourselves
Our families
Our communities
Our valiant, vigilant femme groups
And our valor can feel harmful.

The truth so quickly turns
And the microphone is stolen just as often
As people who won't hear will deny...
Our voices
Our honesty
Our unity.

We gain nothing by exposing monsters
This is for safety
this is for the other woman.
This is what we wish so often

Would never happen to a single person.
Not again.

How often will the sword be mightier than the shield?
How much longer?
We say, "no more."
We say, "no longer."

With unconditional love
With voices rightfully ours
And with the power to empower
We continue on for one another.

ode to teotihuacan

and I didn't like the people,
they were analyzing all my sins
they were from a place that
made them so ravenous they
Feasted on your face and your
newness. And I couldn't find my way
in a city pre-existing conquest...
And I couldn't find my place
because I was conquered...
With the magic in my spine, I
overcame two pyramids
and they say pregnant women can't
climb it when they are the
most valiant humans alive.

And so, I took each ancient step
on rocks where men were sacrificed
with each step rose higher
to the altitudes of liberty
with my ancestors who predicted
their own demise.

"And I listened to my new flesh,"
encasing my growing body
where I morphed into ability
and freed my mind from all anxiety.

How many sons had been born on this
pyramid? Where had they learned the
strength? Who taught them how to
morph on the pyramid of the Sun? How
could they build so high, then vanish
from the earth?

Stars who shine bright explode

Star too bright
you are not forgotten
Your brother mentions you often
You are still big brother
watching over now, like then.

You shifted from mortal
To eternal
with the churning of the River
that houses your ashes.

So bright, you exploded —
Disintegrated back to dust.
You form a new meaning now.
You live on through us.

River is the name
and new birth is the change
the catalyst is you
Still burning
Still flowing

Still above it all.

I feel your subtle movements
you move along with the wind
you push us your own way
if not with body, then within.

In grieving, there is no stopping
In loving you, we're altered
But I know
Stars who shine bright explode.

for she taught me love was abuse

My mother is an obstacle
and my journey is overcoming.
She has always been a clever torment
often keeping my knowledge dormant.

My mother is my teacher
And the lessons bestowed are betrayals.
"It is my right to remember"
all the painful abuse hidden in crevices.

I am my own protector and
healing happens alone in the
comfort of your own self-soothing

And each time you remember,
with your body wracked
Moving tears
Like child wailing
Child in shock, deep inside
Reliving the past.

Mother, you are not welcome
in this chapter
And your removal signals my unburdening

of your anger
of your madness
of your deeply hidden
neurotic
sadness

Mother, I am healing
I am my own
Free woman
I am my protector
I decide what's right for me.

"It is my right to remember"
somberly, achily,
with my whole body,
You are not welcome in this chapter.

Interstitial in your life

I have loved every single kind of you

in your transformative curiosities

Each epoch drives me to insanity

My discouraged self-consciousness snarls

At you.

In brevity,

you are mine and not.

And that is what I love the most. For closer

counterparts cannot exist

And "your kiss is my kiss,"

Breathing for each other is another wonder.

We have been this

Close

So our cells have combined and now we both live on.

We have never been closer since.

And at a distance, there's aloofness in the everyday

manner of your smile. By the instant, you've gone and

now we are so far.

It's haphazard, this wanting and not wanting

This breathing in and then holding your breath.

menstruación

Venimos de la sangre

A la sangre regresaremos

Que no se te olvide

Que siempre vendrás de

la muxer

Que nunca te perdonen

las muxeres que has hecho sangrar

y si te da asco la menstruación

A mí me da asco tu existir

Cuando la sangre se mezcla con la de mamá al nacer —

realicemos el poder del femenino.

Nacemos, sangramos, crecemos

y volvemos a la sangre de la tierra.

En una palabra la sangre es...

infinito.

i miss you, grandma

If I told you sadness could get deeper
What'd you do with the knowledge?
Would you still let children frolic?
If sadness could get deeper, would you swim down
into a darkened crevasse?
Would you explore it?
Would you find it in the finishing touches of her smile?
Would you become addicted to a dose?
Would you look for it again?

If sadness had no end…
would you give in
and go into the cave
would you creep in
and shine a light?

If I told you sadness could get deeper and never end,
would you let it win?

I see because you gave me vision

I've already been in a bed of dust
So forgotten when no one knew there was a fire.
If we could see you now,
Breezing over to shake my core,
I would do it all again. If only
you hadn't let me go
with so much acceptance I turned cold.

You were born to douse me and you
rose at the chance.

But if I could see you now, like
I did back then,
I'd have secrets to tell.
Not like, "you never forget your
First love," no, we know that.
My secret of you, to you, for you, would
be that we keep burning and
Frolicking & destroying it all in
my mind. In our eternal youth
and really only Billie Holiday

gets it as her voice peruses
bookstores we once knew. We
still do. Sometimes I think only the moths keep on the
light, only the spectators
hold the spectacle together. Our
love ghostly and ghastly aflame
and I'm really the only one that's
braggin'... my sopping heart
wet feelings to paper that
everlasting pull for the truth
I can't comprehend... we danced
sometimes, if not alone, then in front of all the moths
who
see. When we did last... when
our fading love tenderly poured
from inebriated lips, you cried
to me. I illuminated your life
you said, raw-lipped, body limp from
pain, to never let this go. From your spell
on this paper I break your word
denounce the bond. And you shook me loose
not far after... I said the end and you
let me go so easily...
Your care, so invisibly there.

adivinando divinidad

Tengo fe en lo divino.
Tengo fe en el amor que
me ha alcanzado en
cada etapa de mi vida.
Tengo un amor por dentro
De mí que me levanta
el espíritu que me guía
en todo momento. Que
me ilumina en todas
direcciones destinadas para
mi. Yo no necesito a dios
para vivir con puro amor
en el corazón y en
cada momento en cada
instante que le doy servicio
A alguien o a mí misma
estoy elevando al universo con
mi poder espiritual. Es por
eso que estoy alineada y
bendecida todos los días.
Me amo, me amo, me
amo, entera, eternamente.

awake at the sight of you

I will always be yours
In my home you roam
In my life, you're right
with my soul, you collide.

I'm limited by my vocabulary
And understanding
And I want to describe you
I want to describe us.
I want to do this justice.

I'll just say this:

>I will always feel this way…
>In my dark solace
>You're my light.
>In my twisted mind
>you quiet the calamity.
>In my love for you
>the world heals…
>When we align, we are divine

You connect my pieces
You see my realness
You're not afraid
You are deserving of
all of me. My years of
longing this sweet
Prolonging all these
years we've waited to
meet... finally
my soul retreats
with you

Into comfort
Into home
Into a love full-grown
Into desire unknown and
all knowing.
Into my heart overgrowing
Into my waters overflowing.

And our lit path
In the same direction
In a revolutionary spirit

Finally connected.

Here's to an undying devotion
A harmonious match
A love so radical
No one's attached

We are together
In beauty
At peace
Towards freedom
At last.

antonio

Maybe I do have to feel
this pain
And I do have to
call you what you are.
I won't call it a break-up
A transition out of
togetherness into
Acquaintanceship.
I will see you around
I will see you everywhere
For a while
It's hard not to want
to see you everyday
It's hard
Some people say good
riddance
Some people say, "I
hate you,"
Some people call men
trash
But I don't…

Anymore.

"We are not well until

we are all well"

"We are not well until

we are all well…"

Ah, well…

I'll say, "I still love you."

I always will

I'll miss you

And let it go

wishing you warmth

all the fun in the universe

endless joy

Infinite happiness

and all the love

ese amor

grande y amplio

Que me diste

Por siempre.

delicate

delicate like a flower?

Delicate like a woman…

a helpless individual

a person who does not know, who needs explaining…

delicate…

delicate rage

delicate fury

delicate timing

Now… when men feel so challenged

when men feel so confused

when they've beat, tortured, murdered…

And still, we're here.

Men with their delicate fear… fear of the delicate.

A man might see a whole garden roaring with life

and reduce it to a flower — something small, so he can understand.

A man would rather consider her a delicate flower, and even say so,

instead of admitting he doesn't understand.

Don't call me delicate unless you want to tempt

Rage, the tempest, my righteous form,

my birth-given right to express myself…

my utter disdain in reminding you:

Women are not flowers.

Delicate like the earth's core.

Delicate like gravity.

As delicate as the shift of power.

delicate like this fist.

On loving myself —

You are so lovely
You love me
You complete me, you make me whole
It's absurd in absolutes the capacity you have
And all your perfection
All your reflections to me are blinding
All of your illogical motives make so much sense.
Sometimes you are that lemonade on a hot day
Sometimes you are sunburnt brown — so
beautiful it's strange
You're an absolute dream
A conundrum in your existence
As nonsensical as your thoughts truly never forming
sense
You don't arrive to a place that needs you
But you are everything
And you've always been
And you've always known it
You own it, so show it.

Waste

I like taking a shit on

company time

It's a waste

I'm a waste

You're a waste

Waste-basket

Basket-case

Why I work in this place

You say it's beneath me

I say it's comforting

Knowing that I operate

Wastefully

Below my capacity

Just enough to be sentient

It's my comfort zone to be

unimpressive

It's got more soul than

Your social media marketing

I'll end on this

Shit.

Mamá

Mamá made me cry
Again and again.
I'd let her die.
You injured my soul
Baby me withered away
There's no one else to blame
You put your hands on me
You're not ashamed.

I don't believe in prison
But they should put you away
Childhood innocence just gone away
And no one around to make you pay.
Just my aching memories on replay
I'll relive it all until your funeral day
And then some.

Child, child, go and play
Free now to love again
Bring me my wings again
Be me, be me again.

We made life

Say I adore you on a prayer
So powerful it's gotten you here
In a future moment
of decay… to be reborn.
Day of forgiveness, a truth
just an essence
A love, just a presence.
I've to look at my life and
demand more here.
Not wilt off casually falling apart
In oceans of your hatred.
Surrounded by deep blue lies…
Your compliments are put-downs
I can see it now as I'm meant to.

question

what's a splash of romance

an eternal, yet daring, lie

a confiscation of individuality

a corny song you play just to play

something dull that can

remind you to forget

a whistle at the right pitch

some cheerleaders on break

they tire of the same, bland routine.

there's more to this life

than philosophers

men regurgitating other men's bullshit…

ad nauseam

an unfinished poem

no thought to contend with.

certain you would've noticed

a blatant death wish

the years you drudged through

you wish had never happened

carried you through torture and disdain

to a moment, you rejoiced in feeling again.

something tepid.

someone tap dancing.

mutual manipulation

I like all the sad boys
that never can commit
Awful of you to admit
your jealousy and possessiveness
A mistake for me to think
I can live like this.

It's taken you this long just to look
me in the eyes
How long it's been since you've stopped
wanting someone else
How patient I have been to let you
feel your feels, when will you allow
yourself to feel something
for me. To feel the need to be
more than just a passing fling.
To stop saying, "we're
using each other." To believe you
can speak for me when we
barely speak between us.

Offering some romance

A proposal to move on
A window into your desire
A love song to hold onto
Sometimes it's a kiss I wasn't
expecting
Sometimes I just miss what the
point of all this is
There's no mistaking a lack
of adoration
No confusion in a union where
we are rarely together
And I ain't even sad
about it, just want the
strength to get up out it.

Nothingness

There's a time and a place for every year.
There are stories to tell that may never finish.

Sometimes, I drink to be lively, but most times I use it to
drown out the city. Sometimes I let myself drown in it.
I'd been locked in a depressive haze.
Every single day that I got up for work was a miracle
and everyday I lied and slept-in was a blessing.
I could only ever keep track of one thing at a time.
I didn't plan for the future much. I didn't believe in it.

I knew that I was just surviving; and that was more than enough.
It was more than I could say for others who were swallowed whole.
I never knew where my ambition had gone
or who I was before it escaped me. I let my desires manage my life…
the thoughts… the ins and outs of them… how nothing and

no one much stayed. How I wanted to be alone, even after the isolation.
How quarantine had changed me forever and how I welcomed
the de-evolution.

Even if I had no drive, I had the desire to live, which was perceptibly
better than when I'd wanted to die. When my hole was so vast and grand
that the day-by-day decision to live, breathe, move, took all my energy.
I never got close to anything seriously suicidal and
I dug a meaning into my skin if anything ever happened.
I gave myself permission to hate.
That always felt like the wrong way to live, but it got me through life.
No one really knew how to treat me and I rather cared for tending to my
old wounds in solitude. It was grasping at ways just to get by, usually by
grasping for a bottle of something poisonous but not

deadly.

I grew tired of wanting pretty and agonized about the meaning,
the meaning, the meaning. I championed the nothingness.
It's more honest than most things, as it's closer to the truth than not.
Aimlessness is a direction.
Derelicts can teach you more than you think.
How can you have a home if you don't have a self?

acknowledgements

First and foremost, for my son, River. We never know where life may take us. I pray to be by your side for a long, long life. It took me 11 years to believe in myself, to finally finish this. Don't wait so long on your dreams. And for my lovers & haters... Lovers, I put pieces of you in here. For some, I call you by name for the last time. Thank you for the memories & inspiration. I mean every word. Sweet haters, it's funny to see you here still keeping tabs. Thanks for the motivation. To my students, you are dear to me, your future inspires me to teach. Grandma Bertha, Nana, and abuelito, I thank you for your hand in raising me. Tia Gemita, Nina, Nino, Tia Marta and all my cousins, thank you. To my parents, for life. Mom, thank you for the ample trauma to choose from. Miguel, you are more my family than most. Your support has been everything. To all my teachers, Mrs. Saldaña, you taught me to read & I'll never forget it. To all my friends, future, past & present, you have been truer than family & every moment I cherish more than you know. Namely, Rachel Sanoff, Nicole Romaneschi, Adrian Acosta, Cassandra Arellano, Zo Shay, Amalia Gustin, Chili Corder, Jessica Nascimento, Geovani Arevalo, and many more I'm sad to have left out. Thank you to my editor Roxanna Campos Nava. To my friends in New York. To my writer friends. To my ex-friends, I'm not over it, don't reach out. Thank you Las Lunas Locas, VONA, and anyone who resonated with my poetry before I had the bravery to create this book.

www.ingramcontent.com/pod-product-compliance
Lightning Source LLC
Chambersburg PA
CBHW060417090426
42734CB00011B/2341